The World Began
With Yes

Also by Erica Jong

POETRY
Love Comes First
Becoming Light: New and Selected
Ordinary Miracles
At the Edge of the Body
Loveroot
Half-Lives
Fruits & Vegetables

FICTION
Fear of Dying
Sappho's Leap
Inventing Memory
Any Woman's Blues
Shylock's Daughter
Parachutes & Kisses
Fanny: Being the True History of the Adventures of Fanny Hackabout-Jones
How to Save Your Own Life
Fear of Flying

OTHER WORKS
A Letter to the President
Sugar in My Bowl: Real Women Write About Real Sex
Seducing the Demon: Writing for My Life
What Do Women Want? Bread, Roses, Sex, Power
Fear of Fifty: A Mid-Life Memoir
The Devil at Large: Erica Jong on Henry Miller
Megan's Book of Divorce
Megan's Two Houses
Witches

The World Began With Yes

New Poems

ERICA JONG

Red Hen Press | *Pasadena, CA*

Book design by Mark E. Cull

Library of Congress Cataloging-in-Publication Data
Names: Jong, Erica, author.
Title: The world began with yes : new poems / Erica Jong.
Description: First edition. | Pasadena, CA : Red Hen Press, [2019]
Identifiers: LCCN 2018039362 | ISBN 9781597098465 (tradepaper)
Classification: LCC PS3560.O56 A6 2019 | DDC 811/.54—dc23
LC record available at https://lccn.loc.gov/2018039362

The National Endowment for the Arts, the Los Angeles County Arts Commission, the Ahmanson Foundation, the Dwight Stuart Youth Fund, the Max Factor Family Foundation, the Pasadena Tournament of Roses Foundation, the Pasadena Arts & Culture Commission and the City of Pasadena Cultural Affairs Division, the City of Los Angeles Department of Cultural Affairs, the Audrey & Sydney Irmas Charitable Foundation, the Kinder Morgan Foundation, the Allergan Foundation, and the Riordan Foundation partially support Red Hen Press.

First Edition
Published by Red Hen Press
www.redhen.org

To my granddaughter, Beatrice—
Who calls herself Bette.

Contents

The World Began With Yes 13

The Breathing Of The World 15

Child On The Beach 16

Oracle Of Light 18

Unicorns 20

Acupuncturist 25

News 26

Blue Bird, Red Bird 27

Child's Play 28

"Be Careful Darkness" 29

Day Of Atonement 30

Brief Valentine 32

Connoisseur Of Longing 33

Hats 34

Inside Out 36

One 37

Love To His Soul 38

New Theory Of Love 40

Where The Poem Comes From— 41

Emily's Birthday 42

Emily Dickinson: A New Daguerreotype 44

Poetry Is Better Than Xanax 46

Spanking 48

Visible/Invisible   50

Why I Hate The News   52

Your Eggs   54

Writing Poetry Again   55

The Mental Traveller   65

The Danish Poet   66

What Is Love?   68

Facebook Friend   69

Not A Bot   70

On Hearing That Alice Munro Is Now A Stamp   71

The Wish Not Heard   72

Breasts   74

Dying Is Not Black   76

Almost Dying   78

Not With A Bang But A Whimper   80

The World   84

Her Death   85

Taking The Train   86

Prophet's Storm   87

Speaking With The Dead   88

Breath's End   90

*The World Began
With Yes*

Everything in the world began with a yes.
—Clarice Lispector

Have you not heard of my universal fame?
I am nobody, nobody, nobody.
—Rumi

The World Began With Yes

One molecule said yes to another molecule and life was born.
—Clarice Lispector

It was always *yes, sí, da, ja*
the sibilant sound of assent,
the slippery tongue in the mouth
of the lover, the *da* dawning,
the *ja* yelling,
the *sí, sí, sí,* sugary & sweet
between jagged teeth.

It was always *yes,*
come in, welcome, eat me,
merge with me, love,
let's join to make another
little bubble of us
who will seem like us combined
but turn out to be another.

It was always lust
not to be lonely,
lust for the apple, the pomegranate,
fruit of desire,
dense on the tongue,
making another you,
another me.

Oh love, eat me, I am yours,
fill my emptiness with joy,
with *yes, da, sí, sí, sí*
let us begin that way
to make a new universe,
soulful, sad, silly,
& full of seas,
seas that are salty
& full of the stuff of life,
me, you, every wriggling creature
we can & can't name
with alphabets as of yet unknown,
with letters that twist & turn
& try to escape the page, the scroll, the rock,
life beginning again
with only a word
of affirmation—*yes*!
Let it begin
& *Be.*

The Breathing Of The World

The world's continual breathing is what we hear and call silence.
    —Clarice Lispector

I hear the breathing of the world,
the muffled screams of the hungry,
the dance of anger in the lungs,
the sharp intake of breath
when danger comes.

I hear the beautiful breathing of babies,
the moaning of mothers giving birth,
the low susurration of lovers cooing like doves,
the leaves greenly breathing of spring,
the snowflakes breathing silent snow.

Breath is what lets us know we are alive.
Breath is love, is affirmation,
is spirit stretching out to bless the flesh.
Breath is blessing. Surely, we are blessed.

Child On The Beach

The Mediterranean is black with bodies
as in the time of the Trojan War
when Homer sang of bloody battles
& heroes lay unburied
beneath the topless towers of Troy.

But this little boy of three
sleeps unburied on a beach.
Where is he from?
The chemical fog of Syria?
The garbage dumps of beautiful Beirut?
The chaos of civilization come undone?

He rests,
his parents lost,
his sisters drowned,
his brother thrown up on another beach . . .

What shall I do
with this dead toddler
who breaks me open to grief?

I will adopt him,
my nameless grandson,
welcome him into my shattered breast,
his death so sweet even cherubs weep
& Nereids float him in their seaweed boats . . .

Little one,
now you are mine—
sleep in my arms while I sing you this lullaby . . .
maybe you'll awaken in a kinder world

where children don't die at the edge of the sea.

Meanwhile, dream of peace
for this broken world.

Oracle Of Light

On November 13ᵗʰ, 2014, the EU landed a spacecraft,
Philae, on a comet for the first time. The journey took a decade.
Puzzled by the name, I looked it up, then wrote this poem in sheer exuberance.
I hope for "Goldilocks' planets"—but can we get to them?

Philae was an island
in the Nile,
an ancient boundary
between rapids & falls,
temple shrine
to Isis & Hathor,
Osiris,
later Christ—
now a spacecraft
taking our spirits
beyond poor Earth.

We are a flying island
that the Little Prince loved,
a seeder of science,
a seer of stars & planets,
an oracle of light.

Air & water
where are you from?
—& we dumb risen apes,
where are we going?

Perhaps Philae
can tell—
An unanchored spacecraft
among the stars,
it is you we love
as we love knowledge
& our need to fly.

Unicorns

Girls love them
even before they yearn
for that twisted ivory horn.

Wistful for what
they never knew,
they braid
the rainbow hair
of tiny Unicorns.

Yet the *Bible*
makes them
symbols of strength.

Were they aurochs
or elasmotheres,
now extinct?

Why did God remind
Job of his own creation
of beasts
when Job was at his
nadir?

Did *Hashem* mean
that animals are stronger

than those who worship them?
You bet!

& Maidens who gaze
upon Unicorns
as Unicorns
gaze upon them
are the fiercest girls
in the red tent.

Come, then, with me
to my own museum
in Paris,
the *Cluny*:
Musée de Cluny—musée national du Moyen Âge,

& see the Unicorn
gazing at his comely Horn
in my Maiden's Mirror,

while she dreams
erotic dreams—
all tapestry—
celebrating
the five senses:

Touch, taste, smell,
hearing, sight.

Our Maiden feeds
both Lion & Unicorn,
forms of desire.

No wonder the
tapestry exults

À Mon Seul Désir!

What more
could Maidens want
than the everlasting
hardness of the Unicorn,
tail upstanding,
supplicant to her

virginity,
hooves in her honied lap,
eating sweetly
from her cupped hand?

Oh Unicorn,
come to me
from your red
forest of love
& drink
my poetry—

The true trace
of my Virginity . . .

Of course
there are more
than five senses!

Knowledge of
Future, Past,
Poetry, Song, Colors,
Stars & Planets.

Stay, fragile Earth
for Bette,
my granddaughter,
that she may know,
the Unicorn of Love
& Longing,
the Unicorn

of Work & Worship,
the Unicorn
of Springing
Hooved Imagination!

The Unicorn
that licks

her little
hand!

That nuzzles
her pink neck,
that kisses
her brown/blue
eyes, that
lies down
with languor
& longing.

Unicorns are
hardly symbols,
but lovers of our
Little Ones!

Gentle, gentle
Unicorn, come
to my study
in the green,
teach my darling girl
to grow
with Fantasy &
Passion,
Plenty & Poetry . . .
That's all she needs.

Acupuncturist

Waiting for my ancient Chinese
acupuncturist
to open the channels of life
or chi, I drink his tea
& admire the frozen river
beyond his window
& free my body to receive
the force that heals or seals
the gifts I've been given
by the dead.

Life comes from death
as we all know
though we are loathe to admit.

Give thanks.
Death is not final
as poetry proves.

News

It is not news that nobody looks to poetry
unless someone dies
or is born.

It is not news
that men are killers and liars
who pretend otherwise.

It is not news
that money shouts
& poverty whisperingly weeps.

The poet weaves a wall of words
against the news but somehow it seeps through.

Blue Bird, Red Bird

For Connie Greenfield, my Co-Grandma, on her Birthday

Blue bird, red bird,
tree of life, twin birds
nesting in our hearts,
we searched for some
marker of your birthday
high above Aspen
& found this golden
weaving of organic
wools & dyes
& thought of you
& your love of life.
The children we share,
& the friendship
of two grandmothers
& grandfathers.
We thought of
your sunroom
with its birds,
we thought
with gratitude
of our children's
love & the tree of life
growing out of
your heart,
the blooming boughs
of chicks
we share.

Child's Play

Max loved animals.
Darwin cars
& Bette babies
wrapped in blankets.
I remember the intensity
with which we loved
our playthings.
They were everything to us
& the concentration we had at three
never to be recaptured.

The mind scatters now,
looking for lost intensity,
looking for the fervor we had as children.
It made us pilfer toys as if toys
could save us.
It made us snatch them from our siblings' hands
as if they would bring satiety.
Mine, mine, mine.

"Be Careful Darkness"

Whitman wrote.
He knew
the claws & paws
of darkness,
how they capture
light & try
to blind
our eyes to hope.

Darkness
at the edges
of our being.
We ourselves are light
pushing aside
the darkness
as we move.

Standing still
lets the darkness
in.

Day Of Atonement

Searching my soul
for deep defects
of character, courage,
carnality, casuistry
& all those other c's,

I find little to atone for
but shopping
rather than charity.
Or shopping
for charity
which is clearly
casuistry of the worst
sort.

Being human
& therefore flawed,
I am surely glossing over
deeper flaws.

Perhaps next year,
I will see my defects
more clearly.
God, grant me
transparency
that great gift
that only comes

when the body
fails.

But my mother—
why am I so afraid
to visit her
as her body
fails?

Atonement
falls down on me
weeping like one
mother- & fatherless
whose eyes
are dry.

Brief Valentine

A hailstorm
on the eve of Valentine's
reminds us we
are not only made of fire
but also ice.

We never tire
of these contraries
which are the spice
of romance
& of life.

Connoisseur Of Longing

You
memorizing passion's moments,
an ornithologist studying birdsong.
Passion's professor,
you study desire,
trying to relive its first moments.
Birds, birds, birds,
their song fills you with longing.
If only we might capture
birdsong in a blanket
as we might capture a bird.

My friend, why be
a connoisseur of longing?
Is that what a poet does?

Hats

A world of hats
& homicides—
old New York—
children playing hopscotch,
painters clinging
like acrobats
to bridges being built—
crime scene photos
where even the dead
wear hats—
everyone in hats!

Peaked caps on workers,
bowlers on bankers,
top hats on plutocrats—
hats everywhere
denoting class—
hats, hats, hats!

Which we have tossed
like sumptuary laws
& yet kept
somewhere secret.

You can tell a king
without his purple,
ermine, or crown.

The world of hats
lives on
in old photographs
& in our hearts.
We still style & file
each other
by cloak, by watch, by ring.
Hatted heads we wear
above our
nakedness.

Inside Out

Why are we
always so ready
to be turned inside out?
Do we crave a reversal
of our power?

Do we chance romance
for an hour,
losing clarity,
simply to devour
forgetfulness?

Forgetfulness
is coming soon enough.
What strength
to remember to remember
while we can!

One

If we could imagine
beyond our body's
borders,
we would remember
our connection
to the sea—
how we gather
& crash
in our saltiness,
how we join
molecule to molecule
in the rush
to be together.

All things
flow & gather,
gather & crash
again—
that is our puzzle,
our conundrum
as we liquefy our passions
& become
one.

Love To His Soul

Love to his soul gave eyes; he knew things are not as they seem.
The dream is his real life; the world around him is the dream.
—Michel de Montaigne

Dreaming my way
into my life,
I live in many houses—
A rough cottage
in deepest woods,
my parents' duplex
full of ghosts,
my grandparents' apartment
opposite that great museum
of fossils & whales,
dinosaur bones
& the shining heavens.

I often move
from hovel to palace
fighting with my father
over money.
My poor dead daddy.
I was #1 on his
hit parade,
which my sisters loathed.
I seem to dream
his dreams
rather than my own.
But perhaps

I have laid him
to rest at last
by moving
to this palace of dreams
full of insistent whispers.

These whispers
are my own acrobats,
hanging on in midair
by their thumbs,
urging me
& my poor dead daddy
to finally (sigh)
let go.

New Theory Of Love

Did Earth steal its moon from Venus? Controversial new theory
suggests Earth pulled the planet's moon away and into our orbit . . .
—Ellie Zolfagharifard, Daily Mail 9/30/2013

We stole the moon from Venus.
That's how love came to our blue planet.
Gravity rules us & love.

We were so close to that other
heavenly sphere that we dragged
its moon into our own orbit,
made it our own.

Ever since then,
we have been ruled by love.

Aphrodite is a tricky goddess,
unfathomable & fond of pranks.
Imagine kidnapping a moon!

But we knew we needed
the strange chemicals of Venus,
the odd elements & smells.

Without those elements
& smells, there can be no love.
Like dogs, we think with our noses.

Or think we think.

Where The Poem Comes From—

a shiver of silver,
trembling sequins across
that mysterious river
at the base of
the spine.

Rapids over
glittering rocks.
Climax of language
like lovemaking,
bringing
peace.

Emily's Birthday

If Emily Dickinson were here,
she would hate
the hubbub,
the twits, their tweets,
the narcissistic fury
of fools & fool masters,
all motley,
all patched & parched
with endless ego.

You follow me
so I follow you.
You publicize me
so I publicize you,
You review me
so I blurb you,
& so it goes.

Money is the root
of all trees
even the ones that grow
poetry & politics.
Just fifty bucks,
just twenty
just two
just one
just fifty cents,

just twenty-five
just two

Oh pay me muse
for poetry,
oh muse,
where did you go?
Why did you go
away?

Emily Dickinson:
A New Daguerreotype

Is that you, Emily?
We have made do
with the old picture.
Hair parted
in the middle,
modest dress,
dun-colored,
inscrutable expression,
not girl,
not woman,
life's taxonomist,
death's rose,
eyes, nose,
fingers that feel—
how irrelevant her clothes,
her hair.

Clad only
in her words,
she is dressed
for eternity—
Beyond fashion,
beyond mortality's reach.
Who cares
how she looked,
looking in?
Not I.

Language
is more than a garment.
It is the poet's skin.
It is hair.
It is flesh.
It is us.

Poetry Is Better Than Xanax

You want to live a life of poetry
even flying across the country
in a plane called Virgin.

You long for the clouds,
the mute, staring moon
to talk to you in metaphor,

reassuring you in this age of anarchy
& mindless destruction that all
will turn out for the best in the end.

I cannot promise that
the sun will not explode
or the moon not wither.

But I can promise that
your poet's dreams
are your flying carpet

past virginity, mortality, despair,
so hold on while your hair
catches fire & fly without fear.

I learned this trick.

Fear is fuel.

Fear is food.

Fear is flame.

Spanking

Yes. I tried it. Or should I say
he tried it—the slap,
the tickle, the nipp nipp nipple,
the tease, the toes,
the tossing rose
with thorns
sans manicure,
sans pedicure,
sans cure.

It never stops.
The wanting,
the wearing,
the wearing down,
the crown
of the head
to the ragged
toes, who knows
why we lust
long past
conception?

We are made
to break each
other's boundaries &
save each other's
skin

for sin
does not exist
unless you insist
on death.

Visible/Invisible

Some say the world
is made of
tiny strings,
dancing lights so
far apart that
endless universes
burgeon & die
in the infinities
between them.

Some say that
parallel universes
(where everything that
happened once
is still
happening)
vibrate in the air.

& some say that
what is invisible
has vastly more power
than what is
visible—& I agree.

Even if we
cannot see
the cosmos

being born & dying,
the miniscule stringlets,
the sharpest fractal edges,
nevertheless they curve
over our smallest moves,
shaping us, pushing
us to explore
the multiverse
in which we thrive
& die.

Invisible space
teams with furies—
life, death, beginnings,
endings—just like ours.

Oh let us make
the invisible visible
if only to prove
our poetry,
our own fierce force of life
shimmering
to eyes
just learning how
to see.

Why I Hate The News

We summoned the gods—
Ares for war,
Aphrodite for love,
Athena for the power
of wisdom.
All the As of Parnassus
bring their blessings
to Z
for Zeus.

We thought
we'd be safe
with these,
safe from harm
but soon we discovered
the fickleness of Aphrodite,
the power-mad grabs
of Ares & Zeus—
Athena could not
save us with
her wisdom.

She lies broken
on the Acropolis,
impossible to mend.

"Didn't you know
not to lean on wisdom
outside yourselves?"
her cracked fragments sing.

Gods crumble.
It's up to you
to put
our wisdom
back together.
You made us
in your image,
after all.

Grandiose, spoiled,
unreasoning.
As Omar sang,

"Tell me then, Who then is the Potter, pray,
& who the Pot?"

Your Eggs

Your eggs,
your mythic daughter.
You can be my daughter
& I will be yours.
Our ages don't matter—
only that we correspond
in poetry after
a hearty breakfast.

Because you remind me
that poetry is
the most delicious thing
I do, you are
my daughter,
making daily life
into poetry, the world
in a shining yolk,
a scrambled white
with butter
all over.

Poetry is
the most important
meal of the day,
without which
we sicken,
we starve.

Writing Poetry
Again

because

it came

unbidden
as it
always
does

thank you
goddess
muse
mary
isis
holy
ghost

aphrodite

we r all
writing
one poem

as anne
sexton
knew
& wrote
me

me too

adrienne

tweeted her
leave-taking

tweets r haikus
or aphorisms
the way i do
tweets r life
(as i write em)

she was brave
adrienne
suffered enough

she knew
her bones ached
her poetry
was enuf

would live
as words do
until the sun
blows up

dear love
aphrodite
maker of all
kidz

tricky
goddess
who
hates
every
1
not bound

2
love

let those
sweet
children live
sour ones too

my grands
darwin
bette
max

your boy

my stepdaughter

named for
dante's
francesca

franny now

no children
r step

trayvon 2

& u
kim
miss you
wearing
ur violet flag

wore
endlessly
the flag of
poetry

poesy
our
only
goddess

hail aphrodite
muse of the
misbegotten

sappho

adrienne

muriel r
sylvia
anne

wystan
will
yeats

you possibly
possibly me

she sings
thru us
a cracked
tune

whistling
down
the ages
like

wind

language
lives
thru
us

not
our
mouths

poppies
fly
there
&
bees

if they kill
bees
we r
done
too

whistling
whistling
whistling
down

down

down

poems
rise
to
cielo

painted
by
tintoretto

&
his
daughter
never
credited

goddess
knows

kim
let us
praise
adrienne
not
weep
her shell
was not
her soul

her soul
in words

fickle
loving

furious
words

aphrodite
worships
language
&
forgives
every 1

by whom
it lives

mr wystan
knew
adrienne
too
&
you

amen

The Mental Traveller

after William Blake

I travelled here & there
looking for wisdom—
in the body,
out of the body.
Until I discovered
my own breath
was the way in
& the way out,
transcendence
& independence
both at once.
As long as we can breathe,
we can be free.
Breath is the magic carpet
we have sought
with too much thought.

The Danish Poet

How fascinating
you are still
writing poetry
though you are no longer young
says the Danish poet
not young herself
& still writing.
As if poetry
could only be love
not death—
breath,
not loss,
a force for spring
not fall
nor winter.

But on winter's edge
you see more clearly—
leaves do not block the landscape.
Sex does
not undo
doom.

You walk
carefully
between the graves,

going to see your grandchildren.
Exuberant, full of questions,
they fill you
with a desire not
to die.

What Is Love?

for my love, KDB

What is love?
Friendship set on fire?
A chess game with no rooks—a fiery queen,
a frozen king, contemplating moves?
Easy to begin—like war—
But hard to end?

Amore regge senza legge.
Love rules without rules—Italians say.
Sunlight on nakedness?
Companionship with juice?
A comedy? A tragedy?
A melodrama?
A satire on human foolishness?

Neediness, seediness, lust, trust?
Two people who combust?
Colliding stars?
Planets fusing at ferocious heat?
Love is all these things.

Love stings.
Love sings.

Facebook Friend

What is a Facebook friend?
Without smell, without taste,
Without smile, without guile.
Is a Friend a friend?

A friend needs.
Seeds you with hope.
Greets you with joy.
You are not a toy.

Not something to count.
A sacred fount.
A friend is proof
You are human.
A Facebook friend
Is another matter.
Proof you can type,
Not love.

Not A Bot

I am not a bot.

Not a figment of some computer's dream
created to sway elections.

I am instead a fleshblood creation
the goddess's typist
tweeting out despair,
trapped between zeros & ones.

Let me out of this hacked computer!
I want to go home!

Kill the bots and their cold computer casings
which never tell the truth & never will.
Give me paper & ink—organic things
that grow the simple flowers of love.

On Hearing That Alice Munro
Is Now A Stamp

I am a stamp.
I who hid in corners scribbling,
I who lurked at the P.O.
waiting for letters that never came.
I who was afraid
of dead letters,
dead children,
dead men
will be collected
by men with magnifying glasses
& sticky fingers.

What does it mean
becoming a stamp
in an age of email?
A relic, a fetish, an artifact?
I am still scribbling,
Goddess knows.
I would rather become a rose.

The Wish Not Heard

You can't wear a wire to hear it,
or a hearing aid,
that wish not heard,
which echoes in your head
wirelessly,
your brain a whispering
gallery of unheard wishes,
wishes like gnats
or cicadas
or even blood-sucking
mosquitos on the tropic
shore where you walk
batting them away
with your bananaleaf fan,
toes in the warm salt foam
of the Caribbean.

Shipwrecked with wishes are we.
Unheard wishes
never to be heard
by any creature.
We grow used to their buzz
in our blood
blessing us with persistent desire.
When wishing ceases
we are done.
Wishless—

only then
we die.

So praise
the wish—whether heard
or unheard. The wish
delivers us,
midwife to the soul,
to wish
is to be alive.

Breasts

I always thought
they were small—
my breasts.

But they filled
my baby's mouth,
& my lover's tongue
loves them,
& my memory is
filled with all
the pleasure they gave
over the years,
 while my mother's
hundred-year-old breasts
still hang
waiting.

For what?
For the tongue
of God?
For the spinning Fates
to release them
into the clouds
so she can remember
how to paint
again?

The sky awaits,
& earth itself.

She used to say,
we all
go back to earth
& become
beautiful tomatoes,
peas, carrots,
cauliflower,
even cabbage.

She was an
ecologist
before the term
was invented.

O Mother
I love you
despite
everything.

Peas, carrots,
cauliflower.
Even cabbage.

Dying Is Not Black

Touch, words, color,
my expiring mother
notices the red & purple of my shirt
with delight.

Color is her language
though she taught me
both painting & poetry,
interlocking languages for her
& now for me.

She has no words for my shirt
but exclaims nonsense syllables
of pleasure, her only brush now
for the ecstasy of red,
the blue note
of mauve over it,
making plum.

Her sounds become
a damson jam
like her mother's,
sweet but muddled.
But her love is clear.

Her love assails
my eyes
as if it were
blood glittering
on a knife
aiming for
my heart.

Almost Dying

Gentled you,
made you kinder,
took away your brashness,
your fear of softness,
you accepted yourself.

My mother has lasted a hundred years
& more.
She sleeps but
will not die.
Her teeth fall out.
She has forgotten
her loud exhortations,
her clever aphorisms,
her screeds
of paint
& poetry.

She shivers on the edge of her death
& will not die.
What is she waiting for?
My father to come back?
God's word?
The forgiveness of her father?
Her heart ticks
so slowly
it could go on forever

while her fingernails
fall off
& her bones
rattle to a heap
on the floor.

At this point,
death would be a blessing.
But
for whom?

Not With A Bang But A Whimper

(My mother died & the world did not end)

How I wish it were
apocalyptically dramatic—
the end of the world.

Armageddon,
burning books of fierce fire,
horsemen with spears,
flaming suns sprung
from trebuchets,
dire projections of our stoned
fantasy lives,
awake, dreaming,
dreaming our dreaming selves.

But no.
Breath slips away
on pneumonia's sweet white wings,
eyes fix on the snowy park & can't see
but a blur of white, eggshell,
cream, buttermilk & smeared smog.

Both parents calmly left
this world of pain.
My one regret was not being

there for Papa, Daddy
as I was for Mother, Mom, Mommy
(as I never called her),
Eda Mirsky Mann the glorious,
great mother of daughters
but no son.

Painter, illustrator, costume-maker,
designer of dresses she could cut & sew.
Designer of *tchotchkes**,
beloved wife, daughter, sister,
who never knew how loved
she was (or did she?),
flirt & party-maker
for her pals,
painters, musicians, actors,
but never crass colleagues
of her husband's trade.

O how she hated *grober yungen*!
Merchants & moneymen
though she adored fur coats & jewelry,
antique screens & silk & first-class travel—
the Trianon Palace hotel
might have been her second home
like poor, headless
Marie Antoinette.

*Yiddish for "a beautiful useless thing," a knick-knack

She embraced her grand Trianon
as the Austrian princess never did.
Poor Antonia,
little nowhere child
of a much too fertile
Queen . . . no Maria Theresa
you—but a fierce
second daughter
of a second daughter
of a second daughter,
like me.

How I mourned my mother
sitting by her side,
saying that I loved her,
crushing all adolescent
ambivalence forever.

I did love her with my crooked heart.
My mother of the crooked heart,
her generosity with flowers & filets & food,
her lavishness with gifts
for all.

I know you adored all three
of us—as we ate up your talent,
devoured your fabulous words,

sucked your bones dry
as daughters do.

One of a kind, my mother,
sui generis,
& generous
to the bittersweet end.

All my love
began with you—
you who left more quietly
than you ever lived.

The World

The world rushes by
people we loved die
& the world does not stop
astoundingly.

We pause
but the world
does not stop.

Her Death

It knocked the foundations
out from under me—
my mother's death.
No surprise but the pain was.
Orphaned like a Dickens hero
& the sky was black as boots.

I should have been ready
but who is ever ready?
I spin in space like a lost
meteorite, looking for the planet
that gave me birth, my Earth.

Taking The Train

Taking the train to the madhouse
as I walk on my treadmill, legs
dream-heavy, trying to walk my way out
of mortality.

Eating fish & raw vegetables, fruits of the garden
the goddess gave but will take away
as I die of hunger like my mother,
fasting her way to 101 years,
but drinking water
& always eating chocolate.

O dearest Eda, my mother, you loved
caviar and foie gras, champagne,
black truffles—nothing that was not costly
& bad for the heart & liver
& yet you lived to 101
& died, slim as
a wraith.

What is the moral of the story?

Eat well, live long, have daughters.
Thank the goddesses—Lakshmi, Fortuna, Juno, Aphro-
dite
Gaia, Persephone, Leto—
for being born a woman.

Prophet's Storm

The head of Buddha
cast in white plaster
melts in the fierce storm
that makes the puppies whimper.

Nothing is left
but his soft smiling mouth.
What he counseled
slides away like wet words.

This is what he taught—not words,
not images, not puppies, nor people
but the manifestation of life
when life is ready.

And death?
As meaningless
as the melting plaster
of a prophet's words.

Speaking With The Dead

Do not mourn the dead. They know what they are doing.
—Clarice Lispector

Speaking with the dead,
I try to hear them
instead of my perpetual monologue.

What have you learned?
I ask.
And they reply:
that we are leaves in a storm,
salt dissolved in the sea,
that a year reduces us
to our irreducible elements
which are speechless in the old way
but full of the sound
an earthworm makes, burrowing,
or a bird falling out of the sky.

No—don't mourn for us in this new form
which admits no mourning.
Mourn for yourselves
and your unlived lives,
still full of questions.

Language, while you possess it,
can heal you.
Take this salve, this balm,

this unguent
with our blessings of silence.

Breath's End

They say
there is a second
at breath's end
where you can pause
your life or not,
a nest where
you can rest
your heart
as if a dart
with poison
at its tip,
could stop your beat,
letting it start again
at will
if you have had
your fill.
I gulp for air
there—not
taking any
chances!

Biographical Note

ERICA JONG is a celebrated poet, author, & essayist with over twenty-six published books that have been influential all over the world. Her most popular novel, *Fear of Flying*, celebrated its fortieth anniversary in 2013. Never out of print, it has sold over thirty-seven million copies in forty-five languages. Erica's latest novel, *Fear of Dying*, was published in 2015/2016. Her books are beloved in Italy, England, Ireland, Scotland, Germany, France, the Balkans, Israel, China (where they are published both in Taiwan and the People's Republic), India, Pakistan, Russia, South America, Mexico, Spain, and Portugal. They are now translated into Arabic.

Her awards include the Fernanda Pivano Award for Literature in Italy (named for the critic who introduced Ernest Hemingway, Allen Ginsberg, Erica Jong, and Jay McInerney to the Italian public); the Sigmund Freud Award in Italy; the Deauville Literary Award in France; the United Nations Award for Excellence in Literature; and *Poetry* magazine's Bess Hokin Prize. Erica founded the Erica Mann Jong Writing Center at Barnard College, her alma mater. It gives grants to Barnard writers.

Erica's poetry has appeared in publications worldwide, including the *New Yorker*, the *Los Angeles Times*, the *Paris Review*, the *Sunday Times UK*, the *New York Times Magazine*, the *New York Times Book Review*, *Haaretz*, *La Republica*, *Corriere della Sera*, *Der Spiegel*, and many other distinguished publications.

Erica lives in New York and Connecticut with her husband and two poodles, Colette and Simone. She often teaches memoir, fiction, and poetry as a guest artist. She loves to teach because she believes that mentoring is feminism. Her daughter is the novelist, memoirist and political essayist, Molly Jong-Fast.

For further information please visit ericajong.com.